"We as a society chose to get more connected, and one of the perils of doing
that is, the more connected you are with
everybody, the more connected you are
with malicious people as well."

—Scott Culp, Manager of the Microsoft Security
Response Center, quoted in "Technology Security Risks
Growing" by Anick Jesdanun, AP, 5/5/2000

"A computer lets you make more mistakes faster than any invention in human history—with the possible exceptions of handguns and tequila."

—Mitch Ratliff

Computer Security

20 Things Every Employee Should Know

BEN ROTHKE, *CISSP*

McGRAW-HILL

New York Chicago San Francisco Lisbon
London Madrid Mexico City Milan New Delhi
San Juan Seoul   Singapore Sydney Toronto

The McGraw·Hill Companies

Copyright © 2004 by The McGraw-Hill Companies, Inc. Printed in the United States of America. Except as permitted under the United States Copyright Act of 1976, no part of this publication may be reproduced or distributed in any form or by any means, or stored in a data base or retrieval system, without the prior written permission of the publisher.

1 2 3 4 5 6 7 8 9 0 DOC/DOC 0 6 5 4 3 2 1

ISBN 0-07-223083-5

Printed and bound by R. R. Donnelley.

Editorial and Production services provided by CWL Publishing Enterprises, Inc., Madison, Wisconsin, www.cwlpub.com.

 This book is printed on recycled, acid-free paper containing a minimum of 50% recycled, de-inked fiber.

McGraw-Hill books are available at special quantity discounts to use as premiums and sales promotions, or for use in corporate training programs. For more information, please write to the Director of Special Sales, Professional Publishing, McGraw-Hill, Two Penn Plaza, New York, NY 10121-2298. Or contact your local bookstore.

To order
Computer Security
call 1-800-842-3075

Contents

☑ *Computer Security: 20 Things Every Employee Should Know*

*G*eneral George Patton and legendary football coach Vince Lombardi died decades ago, but we can learn a lot about information security from them. Specifically, it is about strategy. Be it football, the art of war, or digital security; all of the hardware and software in the world won't be effective unless it is deployed in the context of a well-defined strategy. As an employee of this company, you are on the front line and play a key role in the overall security strategy.

The importance of a security strategy cannot be underestimated. In order to have a secure company, security policies must be clearly stated and available, systems and workspaces must be secured, and employees need to understand what potential risk they pose to the company through the use of their desktop computer, accessing the Internet while at work, working remotely, accessing internal applications, and handling sensitive and important corporate data.

Policies are the primary building blocks for every successful information security effort. Policies provide instructions to you and are used as a reference point for a wide variety of information security activities.

That is where *you* come into play. As a user of corporate information systems, you are on the front-line in the battle to keep the corporate data safe. Just as the corporate security guards ensure that the physical infrastructure is safe and sound, you are similarly a cyber-security guard to the company's digital infrastructure.

While computer security may *seem* like a daunting task, if you follow good computing practices and your computer security policies (which this book is all about), your security mission will be accomplished.

As stated, policy is the key element in securing corporate data. An effective security policy is based on three fundamental security principles:

- **Confidentiality:** the prevention of disclosure of sensitive information to unauthorized recipients.
- **Integrity:** the completeness and soundness of information.
- **Availability:** the accessibility of systems and information to authorized users.

Here are some key points to remember:

You are on the frontline. Employees play a critical role in maintaining a successful corporate IT security strategy. For security to be effective, all staff must be aware of their responsibilities.

Watch out for weak links. Security is a chain where a single weak link can cause the system to fail.

When you work with corporate data, you present a vulnerability to your company. Be aware of your responsibilities for keeping your company secure.

"Effective security depends on a strong partnership between senior management, the corporate security team, and the employees using the systems."

☑ Be responsible and be aware

*I*t's 7:00 P.M. on Friday and Bob wants to leave. The problem is that Alice still has a lot of work to do. Bob has been mentoring Alice, as it's her first week at the company. Alice doesn't yet have a security access card or a user account on the system. So Bob, in his haste to get home, combined with his desire to help a new employee, leaves Alice his security access card and lets her stay logged into his workstation so she can continue to work.

While it might not be obvious, Bob has nearly done the equivalent of giving his credit card to a stranger. Most people would not surrender their MasterCard in such an unthinking fashion; neither should they give over their security credentials.

As an employee and end-user, you play a critical role in ensuring that your organization's security is maintained. The media has an obsession with hackers. But while organizations and the media are busy obsessing about hackers, they become oblivious to the real security threats: insiders.

While it's much more romantic to think about hackers, the reality is that many breaches occur via insiders during normal business hours.

Many of these breaches are accidental and unintentional; others are deliberate and malicious. And if you give people like Alice your access credentials, even with the best intentions, you are responsible. Similarly, if Joe the bartender serves Bob a few too many Heinekens, and Bob then crashes his car into someone, Bob could be held liable for the actions of an intoxicated patron he served.

It all comes down to this: you have your job to do, and security is part of it. When it comes to computer security, as an end-user, you are just as responsible as the chief security officer.

The scenario between Bob and Alice is an all too common one. But if Alice does something wrong, whether intentionally or by accident, it's Bob's user ID that all of Alice's transactions will be traced back to. Bob is not only breaching policy, but he is now liable for any of Alice's actions.

What can you do to avoid this scenario?

Be aware. You are responsible (within reasonable limits) for what happens on your computer and with your accounts.

Know about the company security policy and follow-it. The security experts who wrote the policy did so in the company's best interests—and yours also.

Show consideration for the security policies. They are serious, and breaches can be costly and embarrassing.

"Information security begins with you."

✓ Choose your passwords wisely

Alice is returning from maternity leave as the human resources manager at Duke Industries, leaving her new daughter Winifred at home. With her account being reactivated, Alice now must choose all new passwords.

Alice is so excited about recently becoming a mom she uses her newborn daughter's name as her password to the HR employee database. Unbeknown to Alice, a disgruntled employee, Natalie, has been trying to find out her manager's salary. Natalie downloaded *John the Ripper*, an easy-to-use password-cracking program she found on the Internet. Within minutes, the program checks *every* word in the English language dictionary, as Winifred's account is successfully attacked and its password gleaned, giving Natalie access to all the HR information under Alice's user account.

The above scenario is real and happens far too often. The problem is that people are now required to remember passwords for myriad systems: corporate systems, online banking, voice mail systems, alarm codes, network passwords, system passwords and many more.

As a security professional, I can tell you that most people simply can't choose an effective password. It is a challenge between choosing one that's easy to remember (and ineffective) or one that's effective but difficult to remember.

Since it is so tough to remember all these passwords, people commonly adopt shortcuts; like writing their password on Post-it® notes, sticking them to their monitor or under their mouse pad. Using Post-it® notes is almost as bad as not having passwords at all.

In the example above, Alice makes a poor choice of passwords for two reasons: Winifred is a common word in most dictionaries, and the password *Winifred* can be easily guessed by anyone who knows that Alice is a new mother. The responsibility for catching tools like password cracking software on the network is not the users, but the user must be aware that such tools exist.

Here are three things to remember:

Do commit your password to memory rather than writing it down. If you must write it down, keep it away from your computer and separate from the account name, preferably in a locked or secure location.

Don't share your password with anyone. This includes your spouse or even the system administrator.

Don't use easy-to-guess passwords. Such words or numbers as maiden name, SSN, DOB, the word "password," and so on are easy to figure out. Choose a phrase or combination of words to make the password easier to remember.

"Children are often very clever at guessing or working out what password you chose, and if they can't guess it, they might also be good at finding where you hid it."

☑ *Keep your password secure*

*Q*uick, think of one of the greatest threats to corporate information security. Did you think of internal sabotage, hackers, or corporate espionage? While those are correct, one of the biggest threats to corporate information security is the lowly Post-it® note.

The security problem is when people write down their passwords on a Post-it® note, and then carelessly place it on the monitor, under a mouse pad, or in an unlocked desk. The password is your key to the corporate network and must be appropriately protected. From a security perspective, writing your password down on a Post-it® is unacceptable. Doing this is like leaving your car keys in the ignition. If you do it, don't expect your car to be there when you get back, and you have no one to blame except yourself.

In addition, your password must never be shared or revealed to anyone. Quite simply, don't share it with anyone, not your spouse, friends, or co-workers. If you share your passwords with anyone, you can inadvertently compromise corporate system controls and make activity logs ineffective. The best way to prevent yourself from being improperly held accountable for the actions of another user is to keep your password secret.

While instinct tells us to share and help someone in need, this adage does not apply to the sharing of passwords. If a colleague asks you to give him or her your password, even just once, you must refuse. While it's sometime difficult to say no to a person in need, both the company's computer security, and *your* job security are at risk if you tell someone your password. It's simply not worth it.

Finally, when it comes to passwords, the longer your password, the better it is. Does that mean a password such as rp2(cmAi@v!z is effective? Yes. But, to make it even better, and easier to remember, consider using a *passphrase* such as bottle#shoe or flag9hotel. Such phrases are easier to remember, for you, and harder for others to guess.

With regard to passwords:

Don't ever write your password down and then place it in a public, or semi-public area. This makes you vulnerable to password theft.

Don't share your passwords with anyone. Learn to say no to such requests, no matter how difficult it is.

Choose a long passphrase for your password. That will be difficult for others to guess.

"Your password is just that, yours. Make sure you keep it personal."

☑ Deal with viruses and "malware"

*A*ll *Quiet on the Western Front* is a classic novel about the loss of innocence and idealism. In a similar way, having a computer virus infect your computer can cause you to lose your innocence about the seeming safety of e-mail and surfing the Web. There's dangers out there.

Viruses are one of many different types of malicious software that can cause serious damage to the files and programs on your computer. Viruses are a subset of something called "malware," which is a general term covering types of risks that are intended to compromise computer systems. The main categories of malware are viruses, worms, and Trojan horses, of which there are many different subtypes.

Computer viruses are programs created with malicious intent that attach themselves to other programs. They are capable of copying themselves from computer to computer. They are called viruses due to the manner in which they follow their biological counterpart. Just as biological viruses range from being harmless to lethal, and can quickly spread and multiply themselves; computer viruses can be innocuous, and in many cases, can destroy a computer system or bring down a network, all in a very quick manner.

Computer worms make copies of themselves and travel through a computer network or across the Internet.

A Trojan horse is a malicious software program that tricks users into thinking it is a harmless piece of software, when in reality there is a dangerous program embedded inside another program. When you run the original innocent program, the Trojan program runs as well. Trojans can do things such as steal passwords or take complete control of your computer.

Most malware enters computers via e-mail attachments. Games downloaded from the Internet and file-sharing applications are notorious for containing malware. One of the best methods to protect against bringing viruses into your computer and corporate network is to be very cautious before opening e-mail attachments. If you receive an attachment you're not expecting, especially from someone you don't know, the best advice is do not open it.

Some symptoms of malware and viruses include:

- Computer starts operating considerably slower.
- Files start disappearing.
- Computer fails for no known reason.

And sometimes, there are no symptoms!

If you think you have malware on your computer, don't attempt to fix it yourself. Immediately call the corporate help desk.

One of the best defenses against malware is anti-virus software. Your IT department likely installed anti-virus software on your computer, but don't rely on the software alone. Another important defense is to be very careful about what programs you start up or install on your computer. Here are some ways to avoid malware:

Be conscious of the security threats and viruses. If you're on the lookout for these kinds of problems, you're less likely to be victimized.

Make sure your computer has anti-virus software loaded. Ensure that all downloaded software and e-mail attachments are checked before use.

Be careful about opening any e-mail attachments. This is especially true if you don't know the sender.

"Infections spread because people don't take precautions to protect themselves. Cyber infections spread the same way. Don't let it happen to you."

☑ Use corporate resources only to do your work

*I*n the old days, there was only one thing to do at the computer: work. Now, not only can you work, you can play games, send personal e-mail, chat in real time, work on your resume, and much more.

But corporate computer and communications systems are provided for, and must be used for, business purposes, with *incidental* personal use permitted.

The operative term used here is *incidental*. When the use is *incidental*, personal use is permitted if it doesn't

- consume more than a insignificant amount of resources that could otherwise be used for business purposes.
- interfere with employee productivity.
- prevent any business activity.

But before you do any actual incidental use, make sure to check your company's official policy for the specifics.

Here are a few details about some systems that provide insights to acceptable use:

Telephone: It's in everyone's best interest if employees make incidental phone calls when needed. Calling home to a sick child is perfectly acceptable, and no one would expect one to exit the building to use a pay phone; as that would be counterproductive. But if your child is vacationing in another country, that long-distance international call is clearly unacceptable.

E-mail: E-mail, like the telephone, is simply a medium for information exchange. It is acceptable to send a birthday e-mail greeting to a colleague. But it's clearly unacceptable to include inappropriate language or graphics in that message. Similarly, reminding your friends and family via your corporate e-mail account that it's Aunt Rhoda's birthday is clearly out of the bounds of incidental use.

Also, since these are corporate e-mail systems, there should be no expectation of privacy on your part. While management doesn't make it a habit to review every e-mail sent, they have full privileges to review them whenever needed, without your consent or approval.

Other systems: Whether the system being used is a copier, fax or other type of system; the onus of responsibility is on *you* to make sure that you are appropriately using corporate assets and that the use is strictly incidental.

So when you start to use your computer or other device for some personal purpose, here are some things to consider:

Computer and communications systems are to be used for business purposes. Incidental personal use is acceptable.

Corporate e-mail systems are also for business use only. There should be no expectation of privacy for any and all messages sent.

Respect corporate information systems. If you borrowed a friend's car, you wouldn't go drag racing in it.

"Inappropriate use of company resources can be a way to lose your job."

✅ *Practice safe data transfer*

*W*hen it comes to children, we tell them sharing is caring and encourage them to share their toys with siblings and friends. But when it comes to corporate files and resources, inappropriate sharing just might be the quickest way to security policy violations.

It's important to understand that some information is intended for specific individuals and may not be appropriate for general distribution. You should know which of your colleagues it's appropriate to send messages to and exercise caution when forwarding messages to them or anyone. For the most part, corporate confidential information must not be forwarded to any party outside of the company without management approval unless there is a legitimate business need.

The issue is that while all users work for the same company, not everyone needs to have access to all information. Whether the data is from human resources, R&D, financial, or other areas, information should only be shared with those that have a legitimate business need for it.

This problem is exacerbated by the fact that on average, authorized network users have access to 10–20 times more resources than they need to perform their job and are responsible for a majority of network security breaches. All of these policies are meant to prevent the excessive sharing of files to other users, an activity that often allows users to perform abusive and unauthorized acts.

Overall, access to corporate information must be tightly restricted based on the concept of *need to know*. In this case, *need to know* is for the most part synonymous with *legitimate business need* or *demonstrable business need*.

There are real security and legal risks associated with impulsively sending or forwarding files without first checking whether the recipient, whether inside the company or outside, has a real need to know. The risk is that if confidential information is not appropriately controlled, its possible disclosure, whether intentional or inadvertent, can be injurious to the company.

So when thinking about forwarding information, consider the following:

The productivity enhanced by sending a file may actually decrease security. Be careful before forwarding.

Use the forward button on your e-mail software prudently. Make sure the person has a real need to receive such information.

Know just not what you are forwarding, but to whom you are forwarding it and why.

"Good advice no matter what the situation, but especially with regard to sharing company information with others: think before you act."

☑ Know the risks associated with e-mail

*T*he best way to learn how to deal with e-mail attachments is to watch the bomb squad. While most suspicious bombs turn out to be duds; the potential that they are real requires that they be treated with the utmost caution.

E-mail, to a degree, is no different. While most e-mail is not hazardous to your corporate health; there are sufficient potential dangers to be aware of in its handling.

Years ago, e-mail was simply text messages and nothing more. Now, e-mail software is quite advanced, and with those advancements comes security risks. It used to be that floppy disks were the primary source of virus infestations. Now its e-mail attachments that are the main mechanism used in the spread of viruses.

It's important to know how to safely deal with e-mail attachments to prevent viruses. Executable attachments, those with an ".exe" file extension, are a quick way for viruses to penetrate an internal corporate network, with significant and costly side effects.

When it comes to opening e-mail attachments, don't do it unless you know they're from a known and reputable party. Even then, given that many e-mail viruses use the address book to propagate themselves, they may often come from someone you know who has you in their e-mail address book. If you did not expect an e-mail or an attachment form this person, don't open it, as this may loose a virus onto your hard drive that can do serious damage to your files and end up on the computers of colleagues. So don't assume that because it seems to come from someone you know, this person actually sent it intentionally.

Furthermore, protecting against malicious attachments requires that you keep your anti-virus software up-to-date. Typically, your internal IT staff will make sure the anti-virus software is current, but it's a good idea to check this regularly.

If you do receive an e-mail attachment that doesn't seem to have a legitimate business need, don't open it. This way, you're protected from inadvertently infecting your computer with a virus, worm, or any other type of destructive or malicious software.

E-mail spoofing is another problem. A rite of passage as a kid is making prank phone calls. While they may sound authentic at first, most people catch on. E-mail spoofing is no different, except that it is not always so easy to tell which e-mails are bogus and which ones aren't.

A problem with e-mail is that it is easy to fake. So don't assume the name in the *from* or the e-mail address in the properties field truly identifies the person as these fields can be easily spoofed. Here are some ways to make sure your use of e-mail does not infect your computer:

Understand the risks involved with e-mail attachments. Opening a bad attachment is the digital equivalent of opening a Pandora's box.

Don't open an attachment unless you first know who it is truly from. Know there is a business need for the attachment.

Take heed from the way the U.S. and Russia dealt with each other during the cold war—"trust but verify."

"E-mail is an essential part of business communication, but watch out for those who would abuse this tool, to your detriment and potentially to the detriment of everyone you network with."

☑ Deal with e-mail hoaxes

An e-mail hoax is a message sent deliberately to spread fear, uncertainty, and doubt, and with the intent to generate a flood of e-mail from people forwarding it in ever increasing numbers.

Hoaxes prey on the recipient's lack of technical knowledge and rely on his or her goodwill to perpetuate it. A hoax is comparable to yelling *fire* in a movie theatre when there is no fire. In this case, however, we are talking about yelling "virus" when there is no virus and starting an rapid passing on of the message by all those who receive it, believing it to be the truth.

Perhaps you've received e-mail proclaiming that a virus of some sort has been sent to you unintentionally and it may even ask you to make some modification to your computer software to deal with it. The message also frequently asks you to pass this warning on to others. While such a hoax may be perceived as innocuous, the damage occurs behind the scenes, in the amount of end-user time being wasted, precious bandwidth squandered, and mail server space consumed. It may go beyond that if it asks you to make a change to some file that will affect the way your computer operates.

People forward e-mails because they want to be an electronic Good Samaritan. Yet if each person in turn sends that e-mail to ten people, who also replicate the e-mail, by the time the tenth person is involved, nearly ten billion messages will be sent. From a telecommunications perspective, these e-mails seriously clog networks and interfere with legitimate communications. Many corporate policies prohibit the forwarding of any type of security, informational, or virus warning other than those distributed by officially designated staff.

The two fundamental elements of hoaxes are that instigators use a preponderance of technical jargon and an attempt to establish authenticity by association with a well-known person or organization. Fundamental in most hoaxes is the request to "forward to everyone" you know. Such a request is a pretty good sign you're dealing with a hoax.

Another common aspect of the hoax e-mail is that it will have an eye-catching subject line to grab the attention of the recipient; such as "Warning, Read at Once!" or "Important message from Chairman Bill Gates," and so on. Sometimes the e-mail hoax will be in the form of a chain letter pleading the reader to assist a dying cancer patient or to come to the aid of a financially needy individual.

Here is a good way to find out if the message you receive is legitimate or not: simply type the subject line or the the name of the supposed virus into the Google search engine, and you will quickly find numerous sites that will tell you whether this is a hoax or real.

Let's summarize how to deal with e-mail hoaxes:

Don't forward any type of security, informational, or virus warning. Simply put, it's not your job.

Know how to identify an e-mail hoax. Look for the classic identifiers and red flags.

Deal with potential hoaxes intelligently. Find out if it's real by checking it out on the Internet. Delete the message if it's a hoax. If it's real, check with your IT manager.

"If it seems too good or too weird to be true, it probably is."

☑ Surf the Web wisely at work

As stated in an earlier lesson, *incidental* personal use of corporate computers is acceptable. A few minutes of Web surfing during your lunch break is fine. But when you do this, realize that incidental use shouldn't be considered free rein to visit any site on the Internet. You must use discretion when surfing the Internet with a corporate computer.

Behave towards this surfing as if you were doing it in a public place observed by many people. Some clearly prohibited non-business sites include those that are:

- sexually explicit.
- racist or chauvinistic.
- gambling oriented.

Permitted non-business sites are more a function of your specific organization. While local weather and traffic conditions are likely permitted, more than that is quite subjective. It is better to err on the side of caution than put your job at risk by indiscriminate Web surfing.

Realize that all of your Web activities may be monitored and logged. Even if there are no Web filters, the fact that you went to an inappropriate site will be logged and perhaps noted.

Many Internet sites use cookies, and countless ones require

them. Cookies are files created by an Internet site to store information on your computer.

Cookies can also store personal information (i.e., name, e-mail address, home or work address, telephone numbers, or any other information you provide). Primarily, cookies pose a privacy risk; however, they can lead to security breaches if someone uses your computer. They could use your personally identifiable information for a secondary purpose without your consent.

Finally, never install software on any company computer without first receiving authorization. There are countless programs (such as games) available on the Internet that are tempting to download, install and run.

Many of these programs that circulate the Internet contain viruses. Some viruses (Trojan horses) are packaged inside games and animated jokes to lure you into installing them. Even widely used and seemingly legitimate software may have security bugs or vulnerabilities. Your system administrator may be able to recommend better alternatives or install a supported program with equivalent functionality.

With regard to the Web and security, remember:

Don't do any Web surfing on company computers that you wouldn't do if you were being observed. You put your job at risk.

Be cautious about the personal information you supply to Web sites that require cookies. This may be used for illegitimate purposes.

Don't ever install any software unless you get specific approval ahead of time. It could contain viruses that can damage your computer's functionality and invade your network.

"There's hardly anything you can't find on the Web, but there's lots of stuff that you shouldn't find while you're at work."

✓ Be aware of the dangers of the Internet

*T*he Internet is like the Wild West; a vastly unregulated and free-for-all realm. While there are innumerable good Internet sites, there are plenty that can pose a direct risk to the company and your job security.

As stated in the previous lesson, don't visit any inappropriate Web sites on company time using company resources. Besides these sites, there are other Internet activities that are likely prohibited, such as:

- Use of chat rooms, instant messaging, some listservs (e-mail discussion groups), and other public forums.
- Running your own Internet business on company time or with company resources.
- Connecting a dial-up modem to your computer.

To protect against the dangers of connecting to the Internet in a way that exposes the company's computers and data to outsiders, most companies use security devices such as firewalls, a type of software that helps protect computers from harmful programs of all sorts. If you connect a modem to your computer at work, you are opening a back door that could allow anyone to get access to internal company computers.

The use of chatrooms, instant messaging, listservs or other Internet public forums or e-mailing lists pose both practical and security risks. From a practical perspective, it's easy to get caught up in the world of instant messaging and end up squandering hours and days doing this. From a security perspective, instant-messaging systems can bypass internal security systems and introduce viruses and other security risks into the company's network.

Users often accidentally and unwittingly disclose confidential information via chatrooms and instant messaging. Because of the inherent casual nature of instant messaging, many users lower their guard and may be less than professional in their communications.

Attackers can use social engineering techniques to illicitly obtain corporate confidential information. In these cases, attackers will pose as employees or other authorized persons to gain credibility. Or they may pose as a market researcher or someone attempting to help with the security of your system. While attempting to be helpful in these instant message chats, you may be unwittingly compromising company security by doing so.

Finally, Internet interactions can be recorded and stored for eternity. If these public forums are used to convey information that is either confidential or embarrassing, they can come back to haunt you. People often make embarrassing comments and sometimes even defame other people in instant messaging. Obviating such activities makes for both good corporate and job security.

Let's summarize here:

The Internet is like the Wild West. It is up to you to stay out of trouble.

Don't visit chatrooms on company time with company resources. You can compromise your company's data security and expose the network to viruses.

If instant messaging is allowed, don't disclose confidential information. Remember not to make comments that can later come back to haunt you.

"The Web is a great place to visit, but you've got to know where you're going, or bad things might happen to you."

☑ Secure your laptop for remote usage

*W*hen working in the office, there's security going on, that you may not be aware of. But when you telecommute or use your computer outside of the internal network, the corporate security goes away.

There are many benefits to telecommuting and working off-site. But there are significant risks—physical theft, data loss, inappropriate screen viewing, and more. And this is true for all of your devices, from laptops to palmtops, PDAs or any other transportable computing device.

On systems outside of the internal network, data must be protected in a manner appropriate to its sensitivity and criticality, regardless of where the device is, be it a hotel room or home office.

Don't leave devices containing confidential data unattended unless the data has been encrypted. This prevents confidential data from falling into the hands of unauthorized persons. While a device may be covered by insurance, data whether confidential or not, is invaluable and for the most part uninsurable.

When flying, don't check systems containing confidential unencrypted data. Thieves often wait at baggage carousels looking for laptop bags. Even without the malicious thieves, luggage is often damaged, misdirected, or occasionally lost when checked in. Keeping the device in your possession is a safer approach.

I can't overemphasize the importance of physical security. Besides the devices themselves, all storage media (floppies, CD-

ROMs, zip drives, etc.) containing confidential data must be physically secured when not in use. Also, use cables to secure the laptop to the desk when you walk away.

The shredding of paper is not just for the military. Ensure that any printed matter containing confidential data is shredded. If you don't shred, you may accidentally discard confidential data that can be scavenged by industrial spies. This is known as "dumpster diving" and is both legal (when done on public property) and a successful method for gaining confidential data.

Finally, if you are working in a public place, such as a hotel lobby or airport, your display can be seen from a distance. Ensure that your device is positioned in such a way that other parties can't view it. If you often work on sensitive information, consider purchasing a privacy filter screen, an inexpensive transparent sheet that will cover your monitor and prevent viewing from any angle other than directly in front.

Let's summarize:

Be aware of the myriad data security risks of working outside of the corporate confines. These include theft of both devices and data.

Encrypt important data. This ensures that others won't be able to use it.

Don't forget about physical security. If you look corporate and have a laptop, you are a target. Protect your computer appropriately.

"When using a laptop on the road, you don't have a target painted on your back, but the potential to be victimized is always there."

☑ Make remote access secure

*I*t's not coincidental that frequent travelers are called "road warriors" as it can be a veritable jungle out there, both in the physical and digital worlds.

The advantage of remote access is that you're no longer tied to the corporate office. But the danger is that the security afforded in the corporate office evaporates once you leave the building. Luckily, there are security mechanisms to ensure that road warriors don't become roadkill.

The best way to make sure this doesn't happen is to be familiar with the potentially serious security problems associated with telecommuting and other types of remote access.

First, protect remotely located equipment from theft, and encrypt all confidential data. You wouldn't leave your wallet unattended in a public place or your personal papers visible, even for a moment; don't do the same with your laptop. Everyday, thousands of laptops are stolen. With a little common sense, many of these thefts could have been prevented.

Second, use a *personal firewall* on your laptop. Personal firewalls ensure that your computer is protected from external attackers. If you are connecting remotely via cable or DSL, there is often no security between your computer and the remote site and a personal firewall affords this protection. It can also quarantine potentially dangerous files that are sent as e-mail attachments.

Also, ensure that your remote access passwords are effective. Using easy-to-guess passwords, while convenient, can enable others to illicitly use your account for unauthorized purposes.

Finally, if you're using a modem for external access, don't ever, for whatever reason, use your modem when on an internal corporate network. Any type of internally-based dial-up connection must be routed through a modem pool, which includes security and authentication. Utilizing a modem and not going through a modem pool opens up the internal network to external attacks, and other security vulnerabilities.

If you travel regularly, remember:

Theft is always a potential problem. There are a lot of people looking to steal your laptop, not only for the monetary value of the hardware, but also for the value of the data on it.

When on the road, make use of a personal firewall. It may be your only refuge between safety and attackers.

Don't ever use a modem on an internal network. It exposes your computer to viruses and data theft.

"It's better to be careful than to be sorry."

☑ *Use your hand-held device safely*

PDAs (personal digital assistants) have quickly turned from novelty electronic items with limited functionality to indispensable corporate tools. From hospitals and factories to trading floors, PDAs are ubiquitous and live up to the saying that good things come in small packages.

People often make the mistake of thinking that their PDAs don't need security. That couldn't be further from the truth. PDAs can store megabytes of confidential data and even though they are small in size, they need to be secured just like a full-size computer. As technology advances, PDAs are becoming just as powerful as some computers and have many of the same security risks that PCs do.

In addition, many PDAs now have wireless capabilities that can be used to transmit data. If that data is confidential, it should be secured.

First, your corporate-issued PDA was meant for your use only and shouldn't be lent to others. When you lend it to others, you can't control how they will use it or how they will deal with the confidential data on it.

While your PDA may stay with you, if it was issued to you by the company, it is corporate and *not* your personal property. The PDA was issued to you to perform specific duties to be used primarily for business purposes. If you use it for personal purposes, make sure you do not mind someone from the organization viewing what you've got stored on it. Since the device belongs to the organization, management has the right to do that.

Especially when it comes to physical security, PDAs can disappear in an instant. So make sure you are careful in where you store your PDA.

While the security controls (e.g., passwords, encryption, etc.) on PDAs are not as comprehensive as those on computers, utilize these security controls whenever possible.

Finally, as wireless connectivity is becoming standard on PDAs, that does not mean that the wireless capabilities have to be always utilized or turned on. If wireless is not needed, make sure to disable the auto-connection feature. This ensures that your wireless device doesn't connect to the network without your intervention.

Here are some things to keep in mind with regard to your PDA:

Though small, PDA's require just as much security as a full-size PC does.

Use passwords and encryption on PDA's where available.

Use wireless security when sending confidential data. Then make sure to turn off any auto-connection features if not needed.

"It may be called a personal digital assistant, but think of it as a 'personal business digital assistant.'"

✓ Backup and secure your data

*M*ost people take their hard drives for granted, thinking they will always be reliable and available. Hard drives store gigabytes of corporate data and can retrieve that information in milliseconds. But hard drives are complex physical devices, and it's not a question of *if* they will fail, but *when* they will fail. Fortunately, most hard drives fail after they have long been retired from productive use. But if you have critical information on a hard drive, and it fails, you will have to go to your backups to retrieve the information. Adequate backups enable data to be readily recovered in the event of a hard drive failure.

Even if the hard drive never fails, its enormous store of data must be appropriately secured. If the files and data are not secured or encrypted, unauthorized disclosure of corporate confidential or proprietary data by unauthorized parties can occur.

Backing up and securing your data ensures that critical files are adequately preserved and protected against data loss and destruction. Not performing back ups can, at best, be extremely inconvenient in that it takes a lot of time to reproduce the date which was lost, and at worst, catastrophic as you lose files that you cannot reproduce and that included vital information.

The best time to think about a backup strategy is *before* anything goes wrong. For the most part, if your data is stored on corporate servers, it will be backed up by the IT staff. But you have a responsibility for the data stored on systems not maintained by the IT department. Data stored on standalone desktop or laptop computers are likely to be *your* responsibility to back up and secure. With that, all critical business information resident on your computer must be regularly backed-up.

For backup and encryption of data to work, you must create a backup schedule. It's best to work with the IT department to identify backup resources, file locations, and a backup and encryption schedule.

The backup must be done at a minimum every month. Some types of data will need to be backed up more often, and senior IT managers will make this decision.

Finally, make certain to encrypt backup tapes when they are in storage. Someone trying to find confidential data will likely look at backups as an easy target.

Here are things to remember about backing up your data:

Take care to back up your data properly. It's your responsibility to maintain data that is under your control.

Store confidential information correctly. Make certain that it's encrypted when not in use.

Create a backup schedule for data on your hard drive. Work with the IT department to identify backup resources, file locations and the backup schedule.

"The day your hard drive goes bad, you'll be very happy you have a backup copy of your important files."

✔ *Manage sensitive information wisely*

You might think that terms like "top secret" and "confidential" are for the exclusive use of the government and military; not so. Your company has physical items that it must protect such as computers, office supplies, and the like. Your company also has data that it must protect that's often more valuable than the physical items.

Just as it's your responsibility to secure physical items entrusted to you, so, too, must you look after company data that comes into your possession. This is facilitated by a *data classification* scheme, which provides you with the necessary information on how to handle company information. Classification of data helps ensure that company data is protected from unauthorized disclosure, use, modification, or deletion.

Data classification divides data into a number of different sensitivity categories, each with its own separate handling requirements. Most organizations divide their data into four levels: *Secret, Confidential, Internal,* and *Public.*

Secret data is the most sensitive business information, which is intended strictly for limited internal use. Disclosure is limited to a subset of internal employees for this type of classification. Secret data that is improperly handled can adversely impact the company.

Confidential data is less sensitive business information than Secret, but its mishandling could still adversely impact the company.

Internal data applies to data that should only be used by employees.

Public information applies to information that is openly available to the general public and intended for distribution outside the company, such as press releases, brochures and annual reports.

Data classification entails not only the storage, but also the actual handling of the data. Thus, data must be appropriately protected regardless of its format, be it on a hard drive, zip drive, PDA, printed copy, or even on a monitor.

One way confidential data is often mishandled is when people forget to log off their computers when they walk away. If you are connected to a corporate network accessing protected data, it is vital that you log off, lest someone use your computer for inappropriate activities.

Remember these things about keeping data confidential.

Understand the importance of data classification. It is imperative to the proper and secure handling of company data.

Know the various classification levels. This is necessary for the effective accessing and displaying of company data.

Make sure to log off or lock your screen when you walk away. This is true even if it's just for a few minutes.

"There's a reason for keeping information confidential. It's about protecting the organization's intellectual property and work in process—the output of which pays your salary."

☑ Dispose of digital media safely

*O*ne of the most forgiving features of computers is the ability to *undelete* a file. Even though a file has been deleted, it's possible to *unerase* it. Recovering a deleted file is possible since the system doesn't physically erase the file; it simply marks its storage location as available. Not only this, even if you reformat a drive, much of the data still can be recovered.

The ability to undelete a file has reverse side effects; data that's presumed to be deleted can exist eternally. Just as the backing up of data is critical, it's important to know how to effectively delete files or to completely erase a hard drive. This is crucial to prevent unauthorized disclosure of the data; especially if the media contains confidential information. This is true whether we're talking about a hard drive, floppy disk, Zip disk, or even backup tapes.

If you want to make sure third parties cannot recover deleted data, the best way to do this is to *degauss* the media. Degaussing is done using special hardware and subjects the media to very strong electro-magnetic fields and permanently erases any data found on the storage medium. (Note that degaussing will *not* work on WORM drives or CD-ROMs.)

Another method used is data overwriting or *zeroization*. This involves successive writings of random data on the drive, making the data unrecoverable. This overwriting is done using special software.

The most effective method is the actual destruction of the storage media. Note that for the destruction to be truly effective, the media has to be completely destroyed. It's not enough to simply hit a hard drive a few times with a hammer or drop it on the floor.

This chapter dealt with media that's under your control. However, if another party controls the media or if the files you want to erase are on a corporate file server, there is little that you can do. This is also true for e-mail that resides on remote servers or if your home directory is stored on a remote corporate file server.

When you have to destroy data, remember these items:

Be aware that merely deleting or formatting the media doesn't truly purge it. It can exist for eternity unless it's actively erased.

To effectively and permanently delete a file, you must use special hardware or software.

There is little you can do if the files you want to permanently delete are on a remote server. If it's really important they are deleted, check with your IT department.

"It's often said you can't destroy anything, only change its form. With data, it takes special effort to make this saying true."

☑ It's people, not technology: social engineering

*P*eople often think of computer security in terms of security products. But the main element of security is clearly the *human* element.

Attackers use *social engineering* as a way to manipulate a person's nature to trust others. If someone answers a phone at work, and the other party identified themselves as Joe from accounting, most people would not challenge that fact. Social engineering is basically the hacking of people, persuading them to volunteer information or assistance.

The danger of social engineering is that it invalidates the protection provided by corporate security products and makes your organization vulnerable to attacks and serious losses.

The social engineer's goal is to obtain information that will allow this individual to gain access, and you don't want to be the person who facilitates that. Social engineers will never directly ask for the information; rather they will use powers of persuasion, including a grab bag of techniques including psychological (asking for little bits of information at a time, never in big chunks), impersonation, friendliness, despair, and more. Their objective is simple: persuade you to disclose information to them.

Social engineering attacks occur either electronically (for example, e-mail or instant messaging) or in person.

Note that even seemingly unimportant information may be used as part of a *tapestry* of lies that will persuade someone else to give out the important information. To defeat social engineers you must resist attempts to reveal *any* information that an outsider wouldn't normally know. Even information that seems innocuous could be used to create a more effective social engineering ruse on another employee.

Social engineers succeed by finding the weakest link in the company. Therefore, an important part of prevention is to report any suspicious conversation or solicitation by an outsider. If people suspect they are being socially engineered and they immediately report this fact, then perhaps the social engineer can be defeated.

Keep these points in mind about the people aspect of data protection:

Never give those you don't know company information. No legitimate person or organization will *ever* ask you for your password, PIN, or other similar piece of information.

Never volunteer any confidential information to a person you don't know. This is true whether in person, on the phone, or electronically.

Remember the mantra from the days of the Cold War: trust, but verify.

"You could spend a fortune purchasing technology and services ... and your network infrastructure could still remain vulnerable to old-fashioned social-engineering manipulation."

—Kevin Mitnick
famous social engineer

☑ Secure your work-space

*L*et's now talk about the concept of a *clean desk*, which refers not to neatness but to data security.

A clean desk ensures that when you're not at your desk, sensitive data is properly locked and secured against unauthorized access. It ensures that no inadvertent disclosure of sensitive information occurs.

If you leave your system unattended, make sure it is locked so that a password is required to log in. Implement a screen saver that provides a password lock when the computer is idle for a period of time. And remember to use laptop cable locks to secure laptops from theft. It's also important to secure hard copy materials, electronic media (floppy disks, CD-ROMs, zip disks, and so on) and PDAs when you're not using them.

A clean desk policy prevents those who have physical access to your area from getting any items or information to which they are not entitled. This could be a co-worker or contractor during normal business hours or someone from the cleaning crew during off-hours. Another benefit of a clean desk policy is that items won't be out and susceptible to damage.

Besides the desk itself, make sure that you erase white-boards after meetings if any type of sensitive data is on them.

A clean desk policy is not meant to make you paranoid about keeping your office under lock and key. It's simply meant to make you aware that it's easy for information to leak, and a clean desk policy helps prevent that.

If you are the only one in the area or if everyone in the area is authorized to view the information, a desk does not have to be *clean.* But if you are in a public area, or there are a lot of people nearby without the appropriate authorization to view the data, you need to be more diligent.

Part of a clean desk policy includes making sure that your monitor is not easily viewable to outsiders. Thus, it's a good idea to position your monitor in such a way that people from the outside can't see the display. If you can't do that, utilize a privacy filter device.

Things to remember about a clean desk policy include:

Treat sensitive material like any other type of valuable. Lock and secure it.

Secure hard copies and media as well as your laptop, PDA, and other devices stored in your workspace.

Make sure your monitor is not easily viewed by people walking by your desk. It may display a treasure trove of confidential information.

"A clean, neat desk makes it easier to do your work. More importantly, it makes your data and equipment secure."

✓ Know what to do when things go wrong

*W*ith many things in life, it's not *what* you know, but *whom* you know. When it comes to computer security issues, you need to know whom to call. Your company likely has a group that handles computer security issues, known as the CIRT (Computer Incident Response Team), CERT (Computer Emergency Response Team) or something similar. Regardless of the name, these groups all do the same thing—handle computer security incidents.

If you feel a computer security incident has occurred, it's crucial to immediately call the CIRT. These incidents include everything from suspected security vulnerabilities, social engineering attempts, or theft of data or equipment. Even if you're in doubt, call the CIRT. Don't think of it as being a false alarm; it's simply being vigilant.

The role of the CIRT is to be the first-call incident group and central point of contact for all computer security matters. It's their job to determine if a security problem has truly occurred, to provide damage control and to deal with the appropriate legal and law enforcement officials.

If you get an e-mail about a security issue from an external source, don't handle this on your own. Forward this message to the CIRT without disseminating it further. Security e-mail hoaxes abound, and even though you may be well meaning, you don't want to be the vehicle for perpetuating a hoax or misinformation within your organization. The CIRT can verify the veracity of the e-mail and will be the official disseminator of all such information. This ensures that accurate information is appropriately given out.

Just as important as knowing whom to inform, you need to know whom *not* to inform. Don't publicly disclose any information about internal security incidents to external entities such as the public, media, or law-enforcement (unless you are working with legal counsel).

The CIRT team will have the whole picture and is the appropriate group to speak about security incidents. Often the company might have a very specific strategy when communicating with the public. Any efforts by an employee (however well intentioned) may cause miscommunication and embarrassment to the company.

Here's how to deal with security breaches:

If you think a security incident has occurred, don't panic. Call the CIRT.

Don't try to resolve the incident yourself. CIRT has the equipment and experience to handle this. Your actions could result in destroyed evidence, which may allow the perpetrator to get away.

Don't discuss security incidents friends or the press. The only exception is with law enforcement, when it is necessary.

"It's not your job to solve computer security problems. Check with the pros."

✓ Keep things in context and move forward

*Y*ou may be overwhelmed by the amount of information and computer security responsibilities that you feel you have after completing this book. While this feeling may be a bit overwhelming, computer security will eventually become second nature to you.

But that doesn't mean you should completely relax. Security, like any defense, is about diligence and vigilance. The attacker, whether he is on the battlefield or the computer network, lies in wait, needing but one small break to launch an attack. That possibility, however remote, may lead some people to become overly worried about their day-to-day computer security responsibilities. That is clearly not a good thing, and those individuals need to keep things in context.

Effective computer security, like any other type of security, is not about being paranoid. It's about acting intelligently and consistently with regard to protecting data and computer equipment.

Security risks, like germs, are all around us. Fortunately, most germs are harmless; but some are fatal. So, too, with security risks. Some risks are incidental, while others are so serious as to force companies out of business.

While it's not your job to worry about the risks, it's your responsibility to ensure that you perform your day to day duties in a manner consistent with good computer security practices. The best way to do this is to follow common sense, combined with a healthy dose of skepticism. You don't have to automatically believe every e-mail you receive is authentic, or the people on the phone are truly who they claim to be. Be pragmatic and use prudent caution in matters of computer and data security.

Many a police watch commander ends his or her daily briefing with the counsel of "be safe out there." Such is my counsel to you.

Summarizing your responsibilities for computer security, remember:

Effective computer security requires constant diligence and vigilance. While it's something you don't have to obsess about, it's something you can't ignore either.

Understand the risks and vulnerabilities intrinsic in every computing activity. The more attuned you are to the risks, the better prepared you are to guard against them.

Commonsense goes a long way in both life and computer security.

"Be proactive about security. The job you protect may be your own."

☑️ *Glossary of computer security terms*

*T*his glossary provides explanations of the core concepts of computer security. It is not meant to be a definitive guide nor a complete explanation of the myriad concepts involved with computer security.

Access The ability to view or modify data.

Access control The rules and mechanisms that control access to information systems.

Anti-virus software Software specifically designed for the detection and elimination of viruses, worms and other types of malware before they can perform harm.

Auditing The process of capturing user activity and other events on the system, storing this information and producing system activity reports.

Audit Trail A log file that provides the date and time stamped record of the usage of a system. An audit log can record what a computer was used for, allowing a systems administrator to monitor the actions of every user and can assist in determining if a security violation has occurred.

Authentication The process of verifying that someone or something is who or what it claims to be. It is most commonly performed via a username and password combination.

Authorization The right granted an individual or process to use a system and the data stored on it.

Availability The assurance of the accessibility of systems and information to authorized users; when they require it.

Back up The process of copying files and programs to facilitate recovery, if necessary in the event of failure or loss of the original.

Biometrics The identification of a user based on a physical characteristic, such as a fingerprint, iris, face, voice or handwriting.

Clean Desk Policy The requirement to clear one's desk at the end of each working day, and secure everything appropriately to ensure that sensitive information isn't exposed to unauthorized persons.

Computer Abuse The willful or negligent unauthorized activity use of a computer or network that directly affects the systems availability, confidentiality or integrity.

Computer Security The policies, procedures and tools designed to help protect the confidentiality, integrity, and availability of data and computer systems.

Confidential information Any information the loss, misuse or unauthorized access to, or modification of, could adversely affect the organization.

Confidentiality The prevention of disclosure of sensitive information to unauthorized recipients. It is the assurance that information is shared only among authorized parties.

Cookie A small data file that is stored on a user's local computer for record-keeping purposes that contains information about the user that is pertinent to a Web site.

Cryptography The use of codes to convert data by using a key so that only a specific recipient will be able to read it.

Cyber Crime Any criminal activity that uses network access or computer systems to commit a criminal act.

Data Classification A hierarchical level of security, generally implemented as Top Secret, Confidential, Internal and Public.

Decryption The process by which encrypted data is restored to its original form in order to be usable by an authorized party.

Digital Certificate An electronic credential used to establish the identity of a person or computer.

Digital Signature The electronic equivalent of an individual's signature; used to authenticate the message to which it is attached and validates the authenticity of the sender.

Encryption The process of converting data into an unreadable form to prevent it from being understood by an unauthorized party. To read an encrypted file, you must have access to a secret key or password that enables you to decrypt it. Unencrypted data is called plain text; encrypted data is referred to as cipher text.

Firewall A combination of hardware and software that provides security to a network. Generally used to prevent unauthorized access from external networks to an internal network.

Hacker An unauthorized user who attempts to or gains access to an information system.

Hoax An e-mail message that's untrue and meant to spread from one computer to another by relying on other people to pass it along.

Identification Within information systems, the fact of knowing exactly who you are dealing with on a network.

Instant Messaging A type of communications service that enables you to communicate with a remote user in real-time.

Integrity The level of assurance that the information you are dealing with is complete and authentic, so that it can be relied on.

The Internet A global network connecting millions of computers.

Internet Service Provider A company that supplies a method for individuals or companies to connect to the Internet.

Intruder An attacker who is conducting or has conducted an intrusion or attack against a computer, network or organization.

IP Address The numeric address (i.e., 203.19.49.193) that guides all Internet traffic, such as e-mail and Web traffic, to its destination.

Malicious User A person who has access to a system and poses a direct security threat to it.

Passphrase An alternative to the password that is longer and thus cannot be readily guessed.

Password A string of characters entered by a user to verify their identity to a network or application.

Physical Security The physical protection measures put in place to protect hardware from misuse.

Policy The rules and practices that regulate how an organization manages and protects its information systems infrastructure.

Principle of Least Privilege A core security principle that restricts users to only those functions necessary to perform their jobs.

Privacy At a corporate level, the need to keep data confidential while in transit and in storage. At an individual level, it is the control a person has over the collection, use, and distribution of his or her personal information.

Security The discipline, techniques, tools and policies designed to help protect the confidentially, integrity and availability of computer data, information and systems.

Security Incident An act that deviates from the requirements of security policy.

Social Engineering The art of gaining a person's confidence and having him or her supply you with information you do not have access to. This is usually done verbally by someone impersonating a legitimate holder or the user of the information in question.

SPAM Unsolicited or junk e-mail.

Spoof To make a transmission appear to come from a user other than the actual user who performed the action.

Trojan Horse A computer program that appears to be useful but that actually does damage.

Virus Software that is loaded onto your computer without your knowledge and runs against your wishes. Viruses spread from computer to computer by attaching themselves to a host program.

VPN (Virtual Private Network) A private data network that makes use of a public network, such as the Internet, by encrypting the data passing though it, so that the data can pass to the other end securely.

Worm A subclass of viruses. It generally spreads without user action and distributes copies of itself across networks.

About the Author

Ben Rothke, CISSP, is a New York City-based senior security consultant with ThruPoint, Inc. and has more than 15 years of industry experience in the area of information systems security.

His areas of expertise are in PKI, HIPAA, 21 CFR Part 11, design and implementation of systems security, encryption, firewall configuration and review, cryptography and security policy development. Prior to joining ThruPoint, Ben was with Baltimore Technologies, Ernst & Young, and Citicorp and has provided security solutions to many *Fortune* 500 companies.

Ben is also the lead mentor in the ThruPoint, Inc. CISSP preparation program, preparing security professionals to take the rigorous CISSP examination.

Ben has written numerous articles for such computer periodicals as the *Journal of Information Systems Security, PC Week, Network World, Information Security, Secure Computing, Information Security Magazine, Windows NT Magazine, InfoWorld,* and the *Computer Security Institute Journal.* Ben writes for *Unix Review* and *Security Management* and is a former columnist for *Information Security* and *Solutions Integrator* magazine; and also is a frequent speaker at industry conferences.

While not busy making corporate America a more secure place, Ben enjoys spending time with his family, and is preparing to run in the 2003 Marine Corps Marathon for the Leukemia and Lymphoma Society's Team In Training, the world's largest endurance sports training program.

Ben is a Certified Information Systems Security Professional (CISSP) & Certified Confidentiality Officer (CCO), and a member of HTCIA, ISSA, ICSA, IEEE, ASIS, and CSI.

Andreas M. Antonopoulos, CISSP, served as technical editor. He has over 14 years of information technology and information security expertise. Andreas is currently the global Security Practice Director for ThruPoint Inc. and provides thought leadership to the security practice as well as developing security solutions for ThruPoint Inc.

His career began in the United Kingdom where he was a research fellow for the University of London, researching distributed systems and security and lecturing on electronic commerce. After leaving academia, he founded and managed a security consulting firm specializing in Linux based solutions. His company's main clients were in the financial sector and included some of the largest European fund management companies. Throughout his career he has been involved in teaching and training in the commercial, academic and government areas. Andreas holds a Master's degree in Data Communications and Distributed Systems, a Bachelor's degree in Computer Science and is a Certified Information Systems Security Professional.

"You have zero privacy anyway. Get over it."

—*Scott McNealy*
CEO, Sun Microsystems

"In God we Trust—all others must use a Digital Certificate."

—*Unknown*

Other Titles in the McGraw-Hill Professional Education Series

Notes

Notes

Computer Security
Order Form

1–99 copies	_____ copies @ $7.95 per book
100–499 copies	_____ copies @ $7.75 per book
500–999 copies	_____ copies @ $7.50 per book
1,000–2,499 copies	_____ copies @ $7.25 per book
2,500–4,999 copies	_____ copies @ $7.00 per book
5,000–9,999 copies	_____ copies @ $6.50 per book
10,000 or more copies	_____ copies @ $6.00 per book

Name _____

Title _____

Organization _____

Phone (____)_____

Street address _____

City/State (Country) _____ Zip _____

Fax (____)_____

Purchase order number (if applicable) _____

Applicable sales tax, shipping and handling will be added.

☐ VISA   ☐ MasterCard   ☐ American Express

Account number _____ Exp. date ____

Signature _____

The McGraw-Hill Companies, Inc.
2 Penn Plaza
New York, NY 10121